FROGS AND TOADS

OF BIG BEND NATIONAL PARK

NUMBER THIRTY-SIX
W. L. Moody Jr. Natural History Series

A&M nature guides

Frogs and Toads of Big Bend National Park

Gage H. Dayton,
Raymond Skiles
& Linnea B. Dayton

Texas A&M University Press
College Station

Unless noted otherwise, photographs are by Gage H. Dayton.
On the front cover: Mexican Spadefoot, courtesy Toby J. Hibbitts
On the back cover: Chouch's Spadefoot (top), courtesy Dana L. Drake;
Woodhouse's Toad (middle); Canyon Treefrog (bottom)
In the frontmatter: Mexican Spadefoot (p. ii), courtesy Toby J. Hibbitts;
Canyon Treefrog (p. v); Bullfrog (p. vi); Canyon Treefrog (p. viii); Texas Toad (p. x)

LIBRARY OF CONGRESS CATALOGING-IN-PUBLICATION DATA

Dayton, Gage H., 1972–
     Frogs and toads of Big Bend National Park / Gage H. Dayton,
Raymond Skiles, and Linnea Dayton. —1st ed.
          p. cm. — (W. L. Moody Jr. natural history series ; no. 36)
     Includes bibliographical references and index.
     ISBN-13: 978-1-58544-576-9 (flexbound : alk. paper)
     ISBN-10: 1-58544-576-2 (flexbound : alk. paper)
     1. Frogs—Texas—Big Bend National Park—Identification.
2. Toads—Texas—Big Bend National Park—Identification.
3. Big Bend National Park (Tex.)   I. Skiles, Raymond.
II. Dayton, Linnea.   III. Title.
QL668.E2D38   2007
597.809764'932—dc22   2006029780

This book is dedicated
to two inspiring
young naturalists,
Savanna and Camille.

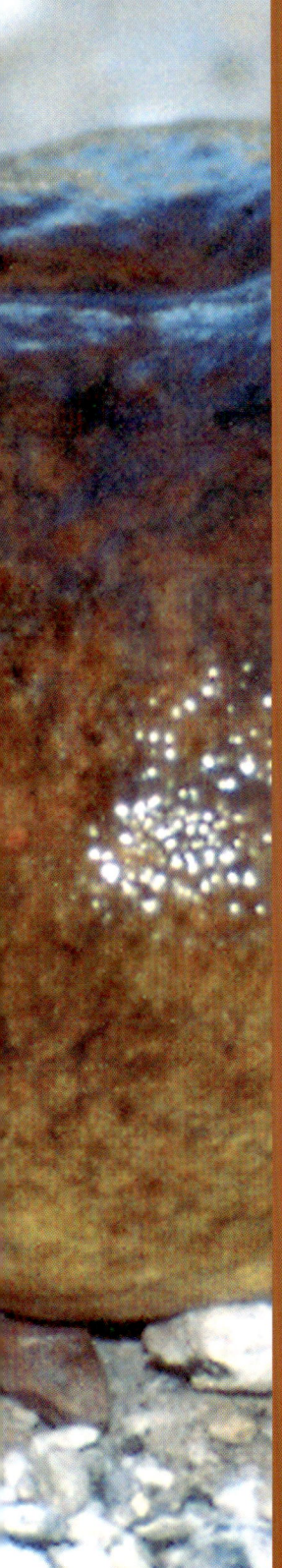

CONTENTS

PREFACE

Amphibians are wonderful. Their complex life cycles, elusive behaviors, songs, and intriguing life-history traits endear them to us. For many of us they are a part of our childhood memories and our education. To think of amphibians—moist creatures who rely on water—living in a desert area such as Big Bend National Park may seem contradictory. But striving to understand the habitats, behaviors, and life histories of frogs and toads that persist in some of the harshest desert conditions in North America is an exciting endeavor. We have written this book for researchers, for amateur herpetologists, and for people who are just generally interested in the world around them. Our goal is to provide a short reference book that introduces the reader to the characteristics and habits of the amphibians of Big Bend National Park.

This book was the result of a seven-year amphibian survey in Big Bend National Park and would not have been possible without the support of the park staff. The entire Resource Conservation and Management Division helped out in one way or another. Interpretative, law enforcement, maintenance, and managerial staff played a large role in helping us locate amphibians throughout the park and constantly kept us informed of recent rain events and pools with tadpoles. We are also indebted to Kevin Bonine, Shannon Claeson, Lily Dayton, Andre de la Reza, Sandy Raimondo, Michele Rosenshield, Wade Ryberg, Eric Wallace, and Stephen Williamson, who hiked the desert flats, slogged through the mud, and drove the roads throughout the night to collect data. Without their support and efforts this work would not have been possible. We wish to thank Dana Drake, Toby Hibbitts, and Ryan Nelson for the use of their photographs and Jim Dixon and Lee Fitzgerald for their mentorship. We extend special thanks to Sam Droege and Robin Jung for initiating the Big Bend Amphibian Survey work in 1998. This work was partially funded by the Amphibian Research Monitoring Initiative and the PRIMenet study.

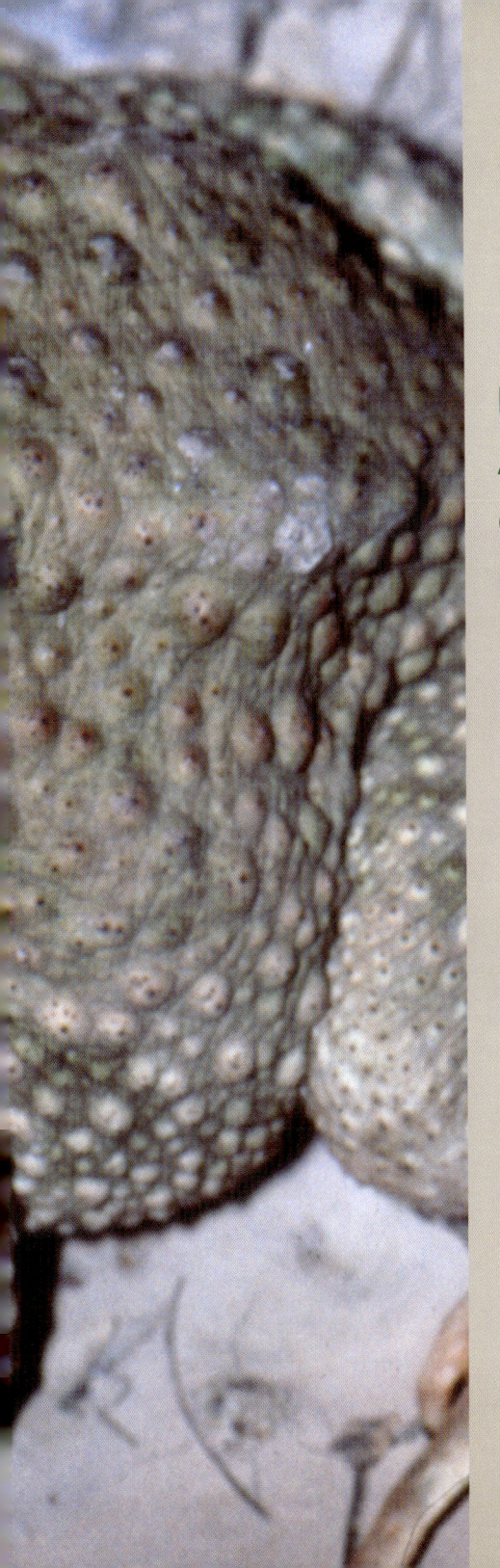

FROGS
AND TOADS
OF BIG BEND
NATIONAL PARK

INTRODUCTION

We have written this book to serve as a quick guide to the amphibians of Big Bend National Park. Although there have been numerous studies on amphibians of the Big Bend region, this is the first guide to the amphibians of Big Bend National Park. It is designed to help visitors understand how different species of frogs and toads use Big Bend National Park's environment and where each species is likely to be found. The book also points out the distinguishing features of each species so visitors can identify the amphibians they see. In Big Bend National Park there have been eleven different amphibian species recorded over the past one hundred years. Two species, the Tiger Salamander (*Ambystoma tigrinum*) and the Green Treefrog (*Hyla cinerea*), are confirmed from single records. The Tiger Salamander was collected in Panther Junction and may have been an escaped pet (native in Marathon and Elephant Mountain).

Green Treefrogs (native to East Texas) were heard calling at Rio Grande Village (likely arrived as stowaways on vehicles). The book goes into detail about specific characteristics that can be helpful in distinguishing the various species, as well as where they may be found, so that you can identify any you may see and perhaps see more than you would without the book. But it is important to point out that all animals in Big Bend National Park are fully protected and may not be handled or harassed in any manner. Enjoy looking!

What Is an Amphibian?

Amphibians are classified in kingdom Animalia, phylum Chordata, and class Amphibia. Within Amphibia are three major orders: Gymnophiona (caecilians), Caudata (salamanders), and Anura (frogs and toads). Most caecilians are burrowers and spend their life in moist soils or beneath fallen debris. They are well suited for burrowing because they lack limbs, have modified cranial features that strengthen their skulls, and have pointed heads and tails. In fact, they look a lot like earthworms. Due to their secretive lifestyle there is very little known about this group, although they are distributed worldwide in the tropics. Salamanders have tails, a distinct head, and limbs (hind limbs may be absent). Salamanders exhibit a wide variety of body types and life histories. Some salamanders are entirely terrestrial; they lay their eggs in moist areas but do not have an aquatic larval period. At the other extreme are species that spend their whole life underwater in caves. Frogs and toads lack tails and have well-developed limbs. Although many anurans move by jumping, many species walk, some species are entirely aquatic and thus swim, and others are climbers (Zug, Vitt, and Caldwell 2001). Anurans are the only amphibians found in Big Bend National Park.

Anuran Life Stages

Before transforming into adults, all frogs and toads go through a larval stage called a tadpole. The diversity of ways in which different species go through the maturing process from egg to adult is one of the many factors that make anurans such an intriguing group of animals. The most common life cycle for a frog or toad is as follows: Adult males call from a water body to attract females, and adult females locate the calling males. The males clasp the females, and the females lay eggs, which are fertilized externally by the males. Eggs develop into free-swimming tadpoles, which then metamorphose into juveniles (small adults); and the juveniles grow into adults. There is a tremendous amount of variation in the way different amphibian species proceed through the life cycle. For instance, the tadpoles of some species are aquatic—they live in permanent water and require several years to reach metamorphosis. At the other extreme, the tadpoles of some species develop entirely within an egg laid on land and do not need water to successfully reproduce.

Breeding and Larval Development

In Big Bend National Park most breeding takes place after

summer monsoon rains during the months of May through September. Shortly after a rainstorm adult frogs and toads make their way to temporary pools, and males begin chorusing to attract females. Some species call from the banks, whereas others call while floating in the water. Females will make their way toward chorusing individual males, who then clasp the females from behind (this clasping is called amplexus). Most anuran species in Big Bend National Park exhibit axillary amplexus (males clasp females near the forelimbs); however, some species, such as the Spadefoot Toads, have inguinal amplexus (the male clasps the female around the waist, just in front of the hind limbs). Amplectant pairs swim throughout the pool while the female lays eggs either on the surface of the water, along the bottom of the pool, or attached to vegetation; fertilization is external. Breeding males can often be distinguished from females and nonbreeding males by the presence of secondary sexual characteristics, such as enlarged, dark nuptial pads on the thumb region or distended, dark-colored throat patches in calling males.

After the eggs hatch, amphibian larvae live similarly to fish in that they breathe through gills and swim using their tails. Most anuran larvae are herbivorous bottom grazers or filter feeders. However, some species are carnivorous, and recent literature suggests that many species are omnivorous, eating both plants and animals, and may derive a significant portion of their nutrition from protein (Petranka and Kennedy 1999). As the tadpoles mature, they develop lungs and begin to gulp air at the surface, grow limbs, and go through drastic morphological changes, eventually transforming into adult frogs adapted for life in the terrestrial environment.

The Big Bend Environment

Big Bend National Park consists of approximately 800,000 acres located in southwestern Texas along the Rio Grande in the Chihuahuan Desert ecoregion. Annual precipitation averages approximately 15 inches with nearly 75 percent of the rainfall recorded at the main visitor center occurring from May to September. Elevation ranges from 1,800 feet along the Rio Grande to nearly 7,800 feet in the Chisos Mountains, with most of the land between 1,800 feet and 3,200 feet. Mean summer and winter daytime temperatures are approximately 91°F and 65°F, respectively, with extremes of greater than 115°F and less than 24°F. The park has a wide range of habitats. The higher elevations of the Chisos Mountains are forested and even have a small population of aspen. This habitat represents a remnant of the Late Pleistocene, when the climate was much cooler and pine and oak forests were abundant throughout the region. Many of the plants and animals that inhabit the Chisos Mountains are adapted to these cooler conditions and can be found nowhere else in the park. In contrast to the Chisos Mountains, most of Big Bend National Park is composed of low-lying desert scrub communities, such as mesquite shrublands, lechuguilla "forests," and creosote flats. Creosote bush (*Larrea tridentata*), lechuguilla (*Agave lechuguilla*), and mesquite (*Prosopis glandulosa*) dominate the plant community over approximately 72 percent of the park (Plumb 1987).

Within these dry, harsh habitats are more than two hundred springs of different sizes that provide essential resources to many plant and animal species. Some springs have water year-round, and others run only part of the year. As you can imagine, these springs are very important habitat for some of Big Bend National Park's amphibians. However, six out of the ten species that occur in the park reproduce in ephemeral water bodies, one species lays its eggs in moist rock crevices, and thus only three primarily breed in permanent or long-lived water bodies. Intuitively, you would think that permanent water bodies are the most important habitat for amphibians in a desert environment. However, even though permanent pools provide the predictable long-lived bodies of water that would seem important for animals with an aquatic larval stage, these sites also provide habitat for both aquatic and terrestrial predators. These predators are very efficient at catching and eating the tadpoles, which makes the permanent sites "death traps" for several of the amphibians that are not adapted to coexisting with predators. Temporary water bodies are less predictable as breeding sites, but they provide a water source that is relatively free of predators.

Rainbow over Cerro Castolon, Big Bend National Park.

Amphibians that inhabit dry areas within Big Bend National Park spend most of their time seeking refuge from the intense sun by hiding beneath rocks and bushes or in holes and cracks in the earth, where they will often remain for several months at a time. The best time to see amphibians in the park is shortly after a summer rain. It is not uncommon to encounter hundreds of toads on a mile-long section of road during the night after a desert storm as they migrate to breeding pools. If you are lucky enough to be in the park during such an event, you will also hear the almost deafening choruses of these wonderful creatures as they try to "beat the environment" by quickly finding one another, laying and fertilizing eggs, and having those eggs transform into juvenile frogs and toads before the temporary pools dry. These breeding events stop as quickly as they begin, so look carefully in the springs and pools you encounter. Perhaps you will see tadpoles at various stages on their way to becoming frogs and toads.

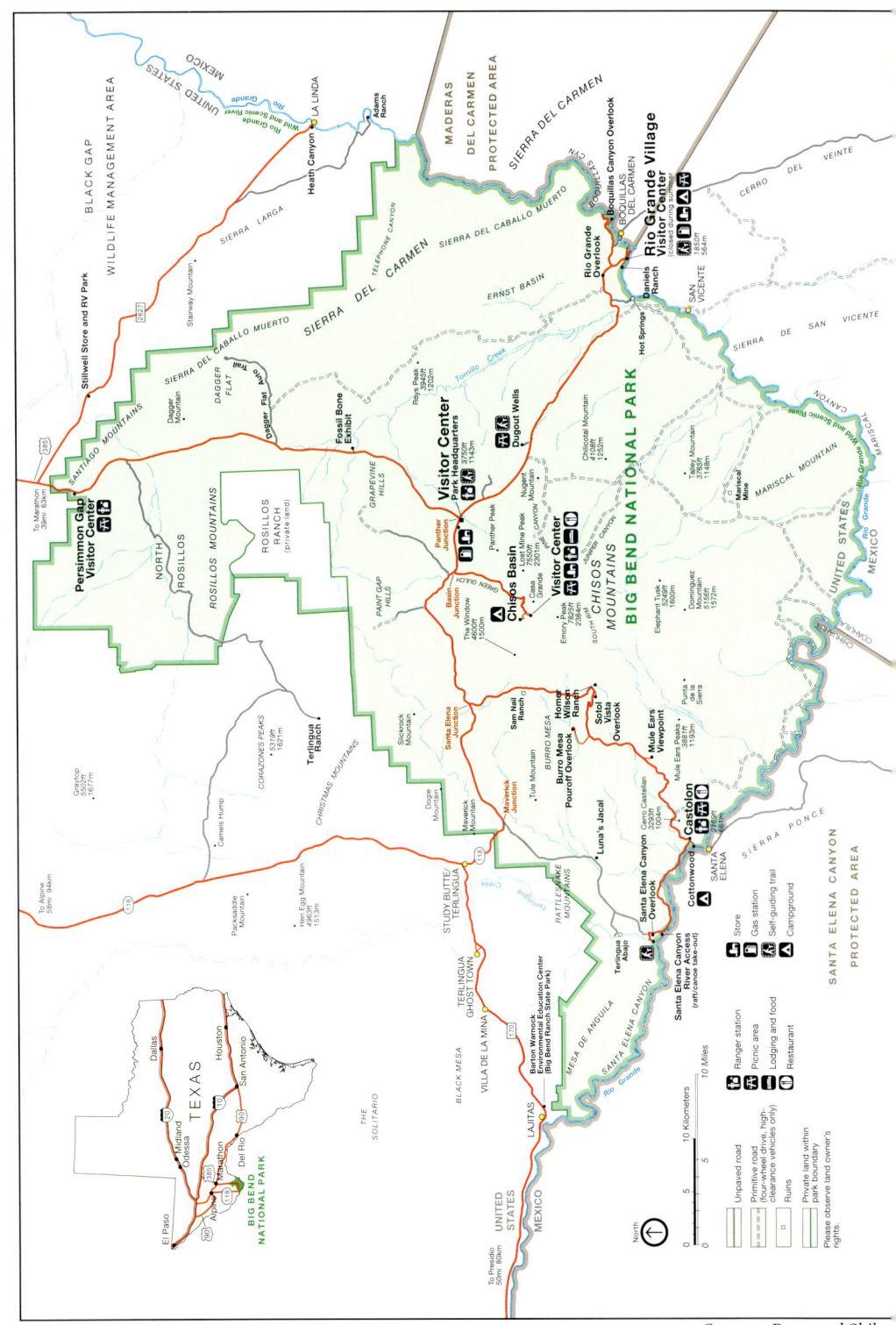

Courtesy Raymond Skiles

TRUE FROGS *(Family Ranidae)*

RANIDS, commonly called "true frogs," have the basic body shape and appearance that comes to mind when we think of a frog, with long, powerful hind legs that make them good jumpers. They typically breed in more permanent water bodies. Ranids occur in all continents except Antarctica and have the widest distribution of any family of frogs. The Goliath Frog (*Con-raua goliath*), a member of the family Ranidae, occurs in western Africa and is the largest frog in the world, reaching sizes up to 12 inches in length (Zug, Vitt, and Caldwell 2001).

A few African and Asian ranid species undergo direct development (from egg to frog without a free-swimming larva). But nearly all of the approximately six hundred species undergo indirect

Long, powerful hind legs help ranids escape quickly from terrestrial predators and move long distances.

Webbed toes help ranids move through aquatic environments.

development, which includes an aquatic tadpole stage before the juvenile and adult frog stages (Zug, Vitt, and Caldwell 2001).

In Big Bend National Park there are two ranids: the Rio Grande Leopard Frog (*Rana berlandieri*) and the American Bullfrog (*R. catesbeiana*). Both of these species can be distinguished from other amphibians in the park by the presence of long, powerful hind legs and extensively webbed toes.

Rio Grande Leopard Frog
Rana berlandieri

IDENTIFICATION: Rio Grande Leopard Frogs are distinguished from all other amphibians in Big Bend National Park by the presence of dorsolateral ridges that extend down their entire trunk. Coloration is typically light brown with several dorsal spots extending from behind the eyes down their entire back. However, individuals can vary from very light brown to almost entirely green.

NATURAL HISTORY: The Rio Grande Leopard Frog breeds primarily in permanent water bodies, but it can occasionally be found breeding in temporary pools. Breeding, as evidenced by chorusing adults and egg masses, has been observed in May through October, December, January, and March and probably also takes place in the remaining months of the year. Conant and Collins (1998) describe the breeding call of the Rio Grande Leopard Frog as a short, guttural trill lasting thirteen seconds or longer. The egg masses are laid as one large clump, often attached to submerged vegetation, and individual eggs are black.

The tadpoles can take anywhere from four to nine months to metamorphose into adult frogs. The variation in larval period

Average body length = 2.5 to 4.0 inches

Rio Grande Leopard Frog *(Rana berlandieri)*.

Dorsolateral ridge

Dorsolateral ridges are characteristic of the Rio Grande Leopard Frog.

seems to be related to local conditions at specific breeding sites. In pools that last longer and have cooler temperatures, time to metamorphosis is generally longer, and frogs are larger when they metamorphose.

Rio Grande Leopard Frogs are not known to burrow in the mud or take refuge under bushes or rocks during dry periods. Although they are not well adapted to persisting in dry habitats where water is rare or sporadic throughout the year, their presence in temporary water bodies that are created immediately after rain indicates they may be able to remain dormant for an unknown period of time near these sites during dry periods. However, we have observed Rio Grande Leop-ard Frogs after big thunderstorms hopping across the desert several miles from permanent water bodies. These observations lead us to believe that these frogs are very good at dispersing and may travel long distances during and shortly after rains. It may be that populations of Rio Grande Leopard Frogs at temporary water bodies represent frogs that have recolonized the pool from other areas rather than frogs that have remained there during dry times.

PARK DISTRIBUTION: Rio Grande Leopard Frogs are common throughout the park and are most often associated with permanent water bodies. They are common at most permanent springs as well as along the Rio Grande; however, they can also be found in long-lived temporary pools and occur throughout Big Bend National Park except in elevations higher than approximately 5,500 feet in the Chisos Mountains.

American Bullfrog
Rana catesbeiana

IDENTIFICATION: The American Bullfrog is the largest anuran in North America. Besides being much larger than other species, it is distinguished from all other amphibians in Big Bend National Park by the presence of a fold of skin (supratympanic fold) that extends from behind the eye to just behind the tympanum (the exposed, round eardrum) above the shoulder.

Dorsal coloration ranges from green to brown with some spotting and mottling. The hind limbs are banded. The *venter* (underside) is typically white with some dark mottling, and a yellow tinge is often present on the chin and hind legs.

NATURAL HISTORY: The American Bullfrog is not native to Big Bend National Park (Dixon 2000). It seems to have become established in the park sometime in the mid-1970s in Rio Grande Village (Skiles, pers. observation). It is not known whether it originally came from the lower Rio Grande where it is native, dispersed down the Rio Grande from areas where it has been introduced, or was introduced directly into the park. It was introduced throughout the western United States during the late nineteenth and early twentieth centuries (Heard 1904),

Average Body Length = 3.5 to 6.0 inches

Bullfrog *(Rana catesbeiana).*

Supratympanic fold

The supratympanic fold in Bullfrogs extends from the eye to just behind the tympanum.

where it was farmed for the production of frog legs. Unfortunately, when demand for legs could not be met, several of the native western *Rana* species were also harvested. This, combined with the fact that American Bullfrogs are voracious predators that will consume anything they can fit into their mouths, has led to a decline in native amphibians where American Bullfrogs have been introduced. There are accounts of American Bullfrogs eating both tadpoles and adult amphibians, vegetation, invertebrates, birds, bats, rodents, snakes, and even small turtles (Bury and Whelan 1984).

Breeding populations of American Bullfrogs in Big Bend National Park have not been thoroughly documented, but calling adults have been recorded primarily during the summer months. Calls consist of a deep, booming "jug-o-rum" (Conant and Collins 1998) that can be heard from great distances. Egg masses are laid underwater, are spherical in shape, and can contain more than 11,000 eggs per mass (Degenhardt, Painter, and Price 1996). Tadpoles require approximately one year to reach metamorphosis.

PARK DISTRIBUTION: In Big Bend National Park, American Bullfrogs currently are known to occur only along the Rio Grande and in the surrounding floodplains.

However, the potential for American Bullfrogs to colonize desert springs and abandoned stock tanks poses a real threat to the biodiversity of native species. For example, if they begin to successfully move inland and establish themselves at permanent springs, it is likely that American Bullfrogs will significantly reduce the park's Rio Grande Leopard Frog populations.

TRUE TOADS *(Family Bufonidae)*

The Bufonidae are referred to as the "true toad" family. There are nearly four hundred species occurring throughout the world, with species native to all continents except Australia and Antarctica (Zug, Vitt, and Caldwell 2001). Toads inhabit diverse habitats ranging from tropical rain forests to the dry Chihuahuan Desert. Four species of bufonids are known to occur in Big Bend National Park: the Red-spotted Toad (*Bufo punctatus*), the Texas Toad (*B. speciosus*), the Western Green Toad (*B. debilis*), and Woodhouse's Toad (*B. woodhousii*). True toads generally have

The Texas Toad *(Bufo speciosus)* represents the typical *Bufo* body plan: relatively short hind legs, warty skin, and compact body.

dry, "warty" skin, and they travel by a series of short hops rather than long leaps.

Bufo species have two metatarsal tubercles on each hind foot and have variously shaped glands behind their eyes called parotoid glands. The parotoid gland stores toxins that serve as a defense against potential predators. Toads do not cause warts on humans; however, the toxins secreted from their skin can cause allergic reactions if ingested or rubbed near one's eyes, mouth, or nose.

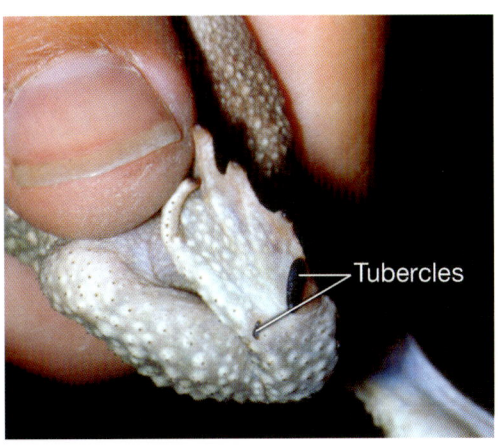

Two metatarsal tubercles present on the hind feet of the four *Bufo* species are used for backward digging into the soil, where the toads bury themselves beneath the surface or vegetation to take refuge during the day or over extended dry periods. Metatarsal tubercles vary greatly in color, ranging from a pale tan to black.

Parotoid glands store toxins that help deter potential predators. *Courtesy Toby J. Hibbitts*

Texas Toad
Bufo speciosus

IDENTIFICATION: The Texas Toad can be differentiated from other toads in Big Bend National Park because it lacks distinct cranial crests, has oval parotoid glands, and has green blotches scattered longitudinally down its back.

NATURAL HISTORY: Like all toads in Big Bend National Park, the Texas Toad breeds during the summer months in standing pools formed by summer rainstorms. Males call from recently filled pools for several days after a rain. The call of a Texas Toad is a continuous series of short, buzzing bursts that resembles the sound of a telephone's rapid busy signal. Amplectant (mating) pairs will often aggregate in groups and deposit their eggs in a large communal mass at the base of a clump of vegetation.

Eggs are laid in long strings and take only about two days to hatch. Tadpoles then require approximately forty to fifty days to reach metamorphosis (Degenhardt, Painter, and Price 1996). During the dry months, Texas Toads take refuge from the heat by burrowing into the ground where they can remain for several months.

Average body length = 2.0 to 3.5 inches

Texas Toad *(Bufo speciosus)*. *Courtesy Toby J. Hibbitts*

PARK DISTRIBUTION: Texas Toads are common along the Rio Grande and in the northern area of the park from Tornillo Flat to Persimmon Gap. Their presence seems to be correlated with locations that are frequently inundated and soils that have relatively high water-holding capacities. These moist soils keep the buried toads from drying out.

Several pairs of breeding Texas Toads are often observed depositing eggs close to one another.

Where Do They Breed?

During seven years (1998–2004) of extensive surveys for amphibians in Big Bend National Park, we have located fewer than fifteen breeding sites for Texas Toads. Of these fifteen, most were in the northern regions of the park in the flats near Dog Canyon. Yet hundreds of adults were found during night driving surveys, many of these on the roads near Castolon and Rio Grande Village. Where do these frogs breed? It may be that breeding habitat for Texas Toads along the Rio Grande has been greatly reduced in recent years (see "Missing . . ." on p.31) and that the adults we see are an aging population with few new adults being added. Collecting age data about these frogs should help resolve the question of whether few new frogs are being added to the population or whether breeding animals are just extremely difficult to locate. If there have been significant decreases in Texas Toad breeding habitat, this species may disappear from some areas of the park.

Red-spotted Toad
Bufo punctatus

IDENTIFICATION: Living up to their name, most Red-spotted Toads have red spots on their back. However, the spots by themselves cannot be used reliably to identify Red-spotted Toads in Big Bend National Park because some Texas Toads also have red spots scattered across the back. A more reliable distinguishing characteristic for the Red-spotted Toad is the presence of a round parotoid gland, which is unique among Big Bend National Park amphibians.

NATURAL HISTORY: Red-spotted Toads inhabit some of the harshest desert environments of any North American amphibian species (Tevis 1966). They breed in temporary pools usually formed in desert washes or on rocky slopes during summer rains. Although we have observed Red-spotted Toads breeding in a wide variety of habitats, most sites are in tinajas, where water accumulates from small tributaries and runoff. Breeding males call from the banks and shallows of these pools with a low-pitched trill lasting from one to three seconds.

Average body length = 1.5 to 2.5 inches

Red-spotted Toad *(Bufo punctatus). Courtesy Toby J. Hibbitts*

The eggs of the Red-spotted Toad are unique among those of the bufonids in the park in that they are laid individually along the bottoms of temporary pools. A single female lays from three thousand to five thousand eggs. They hatch in two to seven days, and the tadpoles then take about thirty to fifty days to reach metamorphosis. Because Red-spotted Toads tend to breed in rock pools, tadpoles are often very exposed, with little cover. In the middle of summer, when outside temperatures in Big Bend National Park frequently exceed 104°F, we have observed Red-spotted Toads in water approaching that temperature.

The markings that gave rise to the Red-spotted Toad's name.

Both juvenile and adult Red-spotted Toads take cover beneath rocks and vegetation during the dry periods throughout the year.

PARK DISTRIBUTION: Red-spotted Toads inhabit a wide variety of habitats and can be found throughout the park except at the higher elevations of the Chisos Mountains.

Western Green Toad
Bufo debilis

IDENTIFICATION: The Western Green Toad can be distinguished from other amphibians within the park by its kidney bean–shaped parotoid glands and its green, bumpy skin. When approached, Western Green Toads will often flatten themselves against the ground.

NATURAL HISTORY: Western Green Toads breed in temporary pools formed during the summer rains. They have been observed to breed at the same site as Couch's Spadefoot and the Great Plains Narrow-mouthed Toad. Breeding males call from the banks of pools, with a loud, buzzing trill that lasts for about one and a half to two seconds. Tan or cream-colored eggs are laid in strings on the bottom of temporary pools and take two to three days to hatch. Tadpoles require approximately thirty days to reach metamorphosis, at which point juveniles search for cover in mud cracks, beneath low-lying vegetation, under rocks, or in rodent burrows. During dry periods adults remain dormant beneath cover to avoid desiccation.

Average body length
= 1.0 to 2.0 inches

Western Green Toad *(Bufo debilis)*. *Courtesy Dana L. Drake*

Parotoid gland

Western Green Toads have kidney bean–shaped parotoid glands. *Courtesy Dana L. Drake*

PARK DISTRIBUTION: In Big Bend National Park, although a few individuals have been found along the Rio Grande near Castolon and toward the western park entrance, most of the Western Green Toads occur in the scattered, patchy grasslands of the northern area in soils that are frequently inundated. These patches are thought to be remnants of dense grasslands that might have occurred there until intense grazing by livestock removed the native grass species.

Woodhouse's Toad
Bufo woodhousii

IDENTIFICATION: Although color and pattern vary in Woodhouse's Toad, it can be distinguished from other toads in Big Bend National Park by the middorsal stripe running the length of its back and by the prominent cranial crests above the eyes.

NATURAL HISTORY: There are no records of observations of courtship or tadpoles of Woodhouse's Toad in Big Bend National Park. However, in other southwestern regions Woodhouse's Toads have been observed breeding along large streams and rivers as well as in temporary pools in arid regions (Sullivan 2005). Calling males exhibit a nasal "waaah" that lasts one to four seconds (Stebbins 1951).

PARK DISTRIBUTION: Historical records of its presence in the park date back to the early 1900s, but no sightings of Woodhouse's Toads have been reported in the park since 1975. Intensive surveys for amphibians in Big Bend National Park conducted from 1998 to 2004 failed to detect its presence. All of the localities

Average body length = 2.5 to 4.0 inches

Woodhouse's Toad *(Bufo woodhousii)*.

Cranial crest

Woodhouse's Toad has a consistent middorsal stripe and cranial crests. *Courtesy Ryan Nelson*

historically known for Woodhouse's Toad occur in the floodplains of the Rio Grande, primarily in Rio Grande Village and Santa Elena Canyon areas. Few Woodhouse's Toads have been collected in the park, indicating that its population in the park over the past one hundred years may never have been very high. Woodhouse's Toad typically breeds in temporary pools along creeks and rivers, and thus the reduced flow of the Rio Grande and the decreased number of major flood events, both caused by damming and agriculture, may have played a significant role in the apparent disappearance of this species from Big Bend National Park. The reduction in flow of the Rio Grande has opened the doors for nonnative vegetation (giant cane, *Arundo donax*) to establish itself in thick stands along the banks of the river. As a result, the river is becoming more channelized. Some areas of the historic floodplain are no longer inundated, and the result is a loss of potential breeding habitat for amphibians.

Damming and agricultural use of water have reduced the flow in the Rio Grande and thus allowed nonnative giant cane to gain a foothold. The growth of cane channelizes the river and further reduces seasonal flooding of the surrounding flat areas. Areas now densely vegetated with cane were once likely open floodplains that provided habitat for *Bufo woodhousii*.

SPADEFOOTS   *(Family Pelobatidae)*

Spadefoots are distinguished from true toads by the presence of a single metatarsal tubercle (spade) on each of the rear feet (true toads have two), vertical pupils (true toads have horizontal pupils), smooth skin (true toads have "warty" skin), and the absence of distinct parotoid glands, which are present on the shoulders in true toads. The spades are used for burrowing into soil, where spadefoots remain buried during dry periods for several months. Pelobatids are distributed throughout North America, Europe, and northwestern Africa (Zug, Vitt, and Caldwell 2001); however, recent molecular work has suggested that the two families are distinct and that the New World spadefoots belong to the family Scaphiopodidae, with Pelobatidae being restricted to

Couch's Spadefoot *(Scaphiopus couchii)*, with vertical pupil and no parotoid glands on the shoulders. *Courtesy Dana L. Drake*

Texas Toad *(Bufo speciosus;* a true toad), with horizontal pupil, "warty" skin, and a parotoid gland on each shoulder. *Courtesy Toby J. Hibbitts*

Couch's Spadefoot, with a sickle-shaped spade on the rear foot.

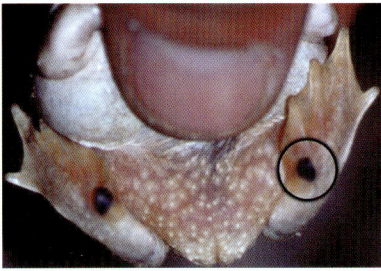

Mexican Spadefoot *(Spea multiplicata),* with a wedge-shaped spade on the rear foot.

Europe and northwestern Africa (García-París, Buchholtz, and Parra-Olea 2003). Until this distinction is officially adopted, we will consider Pelobatidae as the family of spadefoots in Big Bend National Park.

Couch's Spadefoot *(Scaphiopus couchii)* and Mexican Spadefoot *(Spea multiplicata)* are the only members of the family Pelobatidae known to occur in Big Bend National Park. Differing calls, spade shape, and coloration distinguish these two species. Couch's Spadefoots have elongated, sickle-shaped spades and heavily mottled dorsal coloration, and their call resembles the bleat of a lamb. Mexican Spadefoots have short, wedge-shaped spades and no dorsal mottling, and their call is a vibrant trill resembling the sound of a fingernail dragged across the teeth of a comb (Conant and Collins 1998).

Couch's Spadefoot
Scaphiopus couchii

IDENTIFICATION: Vertical pupils; green mottled markings on the dorsal surface; and a single, elongated, sickle-shaped spade on each hind foot distinguish Couch's Spadefoot from other amphibians in Big Bend National Park.

NATURAL HISTORY: Couch's Spadefoot is a burrowing species that remains buried in the soil for much of the year, surfacing only during summer months when monsoon showers create moist conditions. Breeding occurs in the temporary desert pools that form after summer storms. Breeding choruses can be heard from a distance of up to a half mile. The call of the Couch's Spadefoot resembles the bleat of a lamb and lasts approximately one and a half seconds (Stebbins 1985), with males typically calling while floating in water.

Eggs are laid in cylindrical masses consisting of about three thousand to five thousand eggs, typically attached to submerged or floating vegetation. Eggs hatch approximately thirty-six hours after being laid, and tadpoles metamorphose into juveniles within eight to ten days (the fastest of all North American amphibians).

Average body length = 2.25 to 3.0 inches

Couch's Spadefoot *(Scaphiopus couchii). Courtesy Toby J. Hibbitts*

Couch's Spadefoot, breeding.

The accelerated hatching and rapid development of tadpoles enable Couch's Spadefoots to quickly grow large enough to feed on amphibian eggs (oophagy). Couch's Spadefoot tadpoles feed on eggs of both their own species (known as cannibalistic oophagy) and other species (Dayton and Wapo 2002; Dayton and Fitzgerald 2005). This behavior has two potential benefits for these tadpoles. First, eggs provide a rich source of energy that speeds up growth and increases the probability of metamorphosing at a larger size. Second, consuming eggs reduces the overall number of tadpoles that will inhabit the pool, which means there will be more resources per remaining tadpole.

PARK DISTRIBUTION: Couch's Spadefoots are found throughout the park, with the highest densities from Tornillo Flat to the park's northern boundary. Their presence appears to correlate with fine-grained soils that are frequently inundated and retain water. They are rarely found in rocky habitats.

Tornillo Creek running strong after a summer monsoon storm. For most of the year, Tornillo Creek is dry. However, runoff from rains creates a raging river, which usually lasts only a few hours. This photo was taken from the bridge over Tornillo Creek facing west. The Chisos Mountains and Grapevine Hills are silhouetted in the background.

Mexican Spadefoot
Spea multiplicata

IDENTIFICATION: The Mexican Spadefoot can be identified by the presence of a wedge-shaped single spade on each hind foot, tan coloration with scattered red spots all over its back, vertical pupils, and the absence of a parotoid gland.

NATURAL HISTORY: The Mexican Spadefoot typically inhabits grassland and mesquite shrubland habitats. Breeding occurs during the summer months in temporary pools created by seasonal rainstorms. The call resembles the trill made when a fingernail is run across the teeth of a comb and lasts approximately one to two seconds (Conant and Collins 1998). Eggs are laid in clusters on submerged plants or rocks and hatch in approximately two days, and tadpoles require approximately twenty-one days to reach metamorphosis.

Mexican Spadefoots often have tadpoles of two morphological types: omnivores, which eat tiny aquatic plants and animals, and carnivores, which eat larger prey. Carnivorous tadpoles develop from omnivorous types if they have the opportunity to feed on

Average body length = 1.5 to 2.0 inches

Mexican Spadefoot *(Spea multiplicata)*. *Courtesy Toby J. Hibbitts* larger prey items such as tadpoles and fairy shrimp (an invertebrate that can breed in temporary pools) (Pfennig 1992). The transformation from omnivore to carnivore involves a change in dentition, with the new tooth structure and arrangement offering an enhanced ability to prey on larger items.

PARK DISTRIBUTION: Mexican Spadefoots have been found only in the northern part of Big Bend in the plains along the foothills of the Rosillos Mountains. Their distribution outside the park seems to be correlated with open or grassland habitats. There are very few historical records within Big Bend National Park, and this species has not been seen in the park since the early 1990s. Its population may have been reduced as a result of the reduction of grassland habitats in the park thought to have occurred in the early to mid-1900s. Alternatively, this species may not ever have been common in Big Bend National Park and may still persist in low numbers.

Missing . . .

Amphibians are some of the most abundant vertebrates in many terrestrial ecosystems throughout the world. Thus, they are often very important to the structure of natural plant and animal communities, and it is of immense concern that amphibian species have been declining worldwide over the past several decades. Big Bend National Park represents a refuge not only for amphibians but also for other animal and plant species because it has been protected for more than fifty years. However, before the park was established in 1944, Big Bend was grazed heavily by both cattle and goats, and a large number of the native trees were logged for construction. Historically, seasonal summer rains from New Mexico all the way down to Big Bend caused the Rio Grande to flood its banks, resulting in an ever-changing, but predictable, habitat. In several areas of the park, these factors contributed to natural landscape and vegetation communities that were quite different from those we see today. It is believed that before grazing, areas such as Tornillo Flat supported lush grasslands, and the Terlingua Creek drainage once was thick with large cottonwoods. Now the Rio Grande rarely floods, and nonnative vegetation dominates its banks.

To today's visitors the park looks "natural" and undisturbed. But if we look closely, we can see the effects of past changes. For instance, in the Tornillo Flat, look across the desertscape and imagine soils that were several feet thicker, with dense grasslands extending for miles. Today we see mesquite bushes that look as though they are standing up on stilts; their "stilts" are taproots, once deep in the soil and now evidence of the tremendous erosion that has occurred over the years. *Bufo woodhousii* and *Spea multiplicata* have not been seen in the park for several years. The reasons for their apparent decline are not known, but changes in habitat may have played a role.

NARROW-MOUTHED TOADS *(Family Microhylidae)*

Microhylids are distinguished from true toads by their smooth skin and the absence of parotoid glands, and from spadefoots by the absence of spades on their rear feet and an undistinguishable tympanum. Most species in the family Microhylidae live in tropical regions and are found on every continent except Antarctica. In the United States microhylids are represented by two genera, *Gastrophryne* and *Hypopachus,* and three species. The Sheep Frog (*H. variolosus*) occurs only in extreme southern Texas, whereas the two *Gastrophryne* species (*G. olivacea* and *G. carolinensis*) occur throughout the central and southeastern United States. The only microhylid found in Big Bend National Park is the Great Plains Narrow-mouthed Toad (*G. olivacea*).

Several members of the Microhylidae family have a characteristic pointed head that is disproportionately small. *Courtesy Dana L. Drake*

Great Plains Narrow-mouthed Toad
Gastrophryne olivacea

IDENTIFICATION: Great Plains Narrow-mouthed Toads can easily be distinguished from other amphibians in the park by the presence of a distinct fold of skin just behind their eyes and by the absence of a visible tympanum (external eardrum).

NATURAL HISTORY: Great Plains Narrow-mouthed Toads are one of the most widespread amphibians in the park, but their small size and elusiveness make them hard to detect. These toads spend the dry periods of the year taking cover under rocks, beneath vegetation, in earthen cracks, and in animal burrows, where they feed primarily on ants. They are known to live in the burrows of tarantulas, where they have been shown to take refuge beneath the spiders themselves when threatened by predators. The toads are thought, in turn, to protect tarantula eggs and young from infestation by ants (Hunt 1980).

Great Plains Narrow-mouthed Toads breed in a wide range of habitats. Their breeding call, a quick "beep" followed by a high-pitched "Beeeeeeeeee," is very similar to that of *Bufo debilis;* however, *B. debilis* lack the "beep"

Great Plains Narrow-mouthed Toad *(Gastrophryne olivacea)*.

at the beginning of their call. Males typically call while floating in the water beneath overhanging vegetation. Males also produce a "dry call" when calling from a completely dry site. This call is a hoarse, short buzz lasting less than a second. This is thought to be a territorial behavior of males competing for future breeding positions that will be created when it rains.

Amplexus is axillary for the Great Plains Narrow-mouthed Toad, with the male clasping the female behind her forelegs. When individuals are in amplexus, the male toad exudes a gluelike substance from its ventral surface that enables it literally to stick to the female. As with other species of amphibians in Big Bend National Park, breeding pairs float on the surface of the pool, occasionally moving from one location to another, depositing eggs throughout the site.

Eggs are laid on the water surface in temporary pools during the summer months following heavy rainfall. The eggs hatch within two days, and metamorphosis occurs approximately thirty to fifty days later (Degenhardt, Painter, and Price 1996).

PARK DISTRIBUTION: Although Great Plains Narrow-mouthed Toads are rarely encountered, they occur in a wide range of habitats and may be one of the more widespread amphibians in Big Bend National Park. They can be found in open areas with relatively fine sediments to rocky canyon pools.

The Great Plains Narrow-mouthed Toad has a skin fold behind the eye and no visible tympanum. *Courtesy Dana L. Drake*

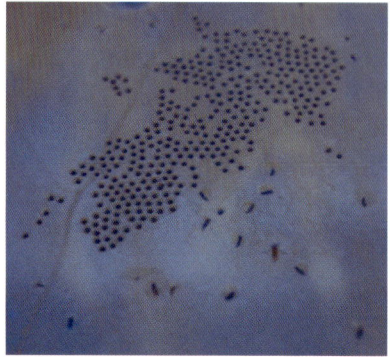

Eggs of the Great Plains Narrow-mouthed Toad are laid individually (but often form clumps) on the surface of temporary pools.

TREEFROGS   *(Family Hylidae)*

The members of the large Hylidae family are often referred to as "treefrogs" because many of the species are tree dwellers. There are more than five hundred species of hylids worldwide, with the highest diversity found in Central and South America. Hylids inhabit numerous types of habitats, including canyon floors, trees, mountain meadows, and coniferous and deciduous forests.

Hylids are generally small frogs with slim "waists" and long legs (Stebbins 1985). They exhibit a wide variety of colors, from the tomato red *Hyla calcarata* to emerald green *Phyllomedusa* spp. Several of the hylids have an extra toe segment, which forms a prominent toe pad that allows them to climb steep surfaces such as rock walls and trees. The Canyon Treefrog (*H. arenicolor*) is the only member of the hylid family found in Big Bend National Park.

Toe pads allow treefrogs to cling to rock walls and other steep surfaces.

Canyon Treefrog
Hyla arenicolor

IDENTIFICATION: The Canyon Treefrog can be distinguished from other amphibians in Big Bend National Park by the presence of toe pads.

NATURAL HISTORY: Canyon Treefrogs inhabit steep-walled canyons where water accumulates during the summer months. During the dry months they often take refuge in rock crevices, where temperatures are more stable and cooler than the ambient environment. Canyon Treefrogs can change color rapidly, enabling them to blend in with their surroundings, with coloration varying from a solid pale brown to a spotted or mottled dark brown and olive.

Breeding in Big Bend National Park occurs primarily in high-elevation, temporary pools in the Chisos Mountains from May through August following summer rains. The call of the Canyon Treefrog is an explosive, broken trill that sounds like a rivet gun and lasts one to three seconds (Stebbins 1985). Males call primarily in the evening, although occasionally during the day, while clinging to rock faces above pools.

Average body length = 1.25 to 2.0 inches

Canyon Treefrog *(Hyla arenicolor)*.

Throughout mountain ranges in the southwestern United States and Mexico, the Canyon Treefrog inhabits canyon bottoms and springs. This frog has smooth, permeable skin and is very susceptible to drying out when it moves through arid environments. As a result, this species seems to be constrained to the relatively cool, moist mountain habitats, and populations of Canyon Treefrogs throughout the southwestern deserts likely represent isolated populations with very little gene flow (Barber 1999). Hence, mountain habitats can be thought of as islands within the desert "sea" (Gehlbach 1981).

Eggs are laid in a film on the bottom of the pool and take approximately three days to hatch. The tadpoles reach metamorphosis in thirty to fifty days. During the summer months it is very common to see Black-necked Garter Snakes (*Thamnophis cyrtopsis*) swimming in standing water throughout the Chisos Mountains, where they feed on treefrog tadpoles.

PARK DISTRIBUTION: Canyon Treefrogs are associated with rocky canyons found primarily in the Chisos Mountains and the surrounding foothills. This species is restricted to higher elevations within the park.

The markings and color of the Canyon Treefrog are highly variable, and individuals can change color almost instantly, making them hard to see.

TROPICAL FROGS   *(Family Leptodactylidae)*

Members of Leptodactyli-
dae compose a large fam-
ily of New World frogs
(more than 750 species) primarily distributed in Central and
South America. Most leptodac-
tylids breed in water; however,
some species build foam nests on
vegetation and others lay their
eggs in rock crevices and other
moist areas. Species that lay their
eggs in terrestrial environments
develop entirely within the egg
and emerge as fully formed frogs
(Stebbins 1985).

Species within this diverse family range from less than 0.5 inch
to more than 4 inches and live in
a wide variety of habitats, including streams, rock cliffs, and trees.
Most species are insectivores, feed-
ing primarily on small terrestrial
invertebrates. However, some species, such as members of the genus
Ceratophrys, are carnivorous and
feed primarily on small vertebrates. The only member of this
family in Big Bend National Park is
the Spotted Chirping Frog (*Syrrhophus guttilatus*).

Spotted Chirping Frogs are nocturnal. They spend most of their life
deep in rock crevices. Their relatively large eyes enable them to see in
dark environments. *Courtesy Dana L. Drake*

Spotted Chirping Frog
Syrrhophus guttilatus

IDENTIFICATION: The Spotted Chirping Frog can be identified by its smooth skin; small, slender body; mottled dorsal markings; and lack of spades on the hind feet.

NATURAL HISTORY: Very little is known about the reproductive biology of the Spotted Chirping Frog. The exact location where eggs are laid is unknown; however, it is believed that eggs are laid in moist crevices, perhaps beneath soil or other organic material. Eggs undergo direct development (tadpoles become fully formed frogs before hatching). Breeding occurs from April through July. The Spotted Chirping Frogs in Big Bend National Park represent a relic population, now thought to be confined primarily to the Chisos Mountains. The closest known population of these frogs outside the park is to the north near Elephant Mountain. Several herpetologists believe that the Spotted Chirping Frog may actually be the same species as the Cliff Chirping Frog (*S. marnockii*), which is found approximately 200 miles to the east of Big Bend National Park (Dixon 2000). Furthermore, there

Average body length = 0.75 to 1.25 inches

Spotted Chirping Frog *(Syrrhophus guttilatus)*.

is uncertainty regarding whether *S. guttilatus* should be in the genus *Eleutherodactylus* (Crother et al. 2000) or should remain in the genus *Syrrhophus* (Dixon 2000). We consider the jury still out on the placement of this species and will continue to use *S. guttilatus.*

Calling typically occurs during the evening after a rain, when conditions are moist and the temperature is between 60°F and 80°F. Spotted Chirping Frogs have two very distinct calls: a short, sharp chirp and a one- to two-second trill.

Spotted Chirping Frogs are hard to locate. Their calls are not very loud and blend into the surrounding desert invertebrate chorus, making them difficult for the inexperienced ear to identify. Even if you can pick out the call, the rocky terrain where Spotted Chirping Frogs occur often makes it difficult to figure out the source of the call, because the sound bounces around from rock to rock.

PARK DISTRIBUTION: Spotted Chirping Frogs are located primarily in the Chisos Mountains on rocky talus slopes and in canyon streams and small caves. There have also been reports of calling individuals along the Rio Grande and in the surrounding foothills of the Chisos Mountains. Because of their elusiveness, it may be that park distributions are actually much broader than have been directly observed and reported.

Spotted Chirping Frogs in Big Bend National Park can be heard calling in the evening, after a spring or summer rain.

DICHOTOMOUS KEY TO THE FROGS AND TOADS OF BIG BEND NATIONAL PARK

Dichotomous keys are commonly used by scientists to decipher what organism they are looking at. The key begins at the top and requires users to choose one of two alternatives at each step. Each step either gives the name of the organism or directs the user to another step farther down in the key. Below we have provided a dichotomous key for the amphibians of Big Bend National Park.

1. Single metatarsal tubercle (spade) on each hind foot 2
   Zero or two metatarsal tubercles on each hind foot 3

2. Green with black mottling, metatarsal tubercle sickle-
   shaped. . . . . .Couch's Spadefoot (*Scaphiopus couchii*)
   Tan with sparse blotches, metatarsal tubercle spade-
   shaped. . . . . .New Mexico Spadefoot (*Spea multiplicata*)

3. Tympanum not visible. . . . . .Great Plains Narrow-mouthed
   Toad (*Gastrophryne olivacea*)
   Tympanum clearly visible 4

4. Parotoid glands present 5
   Parotoid glands absent 8

5. Middorsal stripe present. . . . . . .Woodhouse's Toad (*Bufo woodhousii*)
   Middorsal stripe absent. 6

6. Parotoid gland circular, dorsal coloring gray to brown, often with
   red spots . . . . Red-spotted Toad *(B. punctatus)*
   Parotoid elongate or kidney bean–shaped, dorsal markings
   present. 7

7. Parotoid elongate, dark blotches often present on
dorsum. . . . . .Texas Toad (*B. speciosus*)
Parotoid kidney bean–shaped, body green, vermiculate pattern on
dorsum. . . . . .Western Green Toad (*B. debilis*)

8. Dorsolateral or supratympanic folds present. 9
Dorsolateral or supratympanic folds absent. . . . . .Spotted
Chirping Frog (*Syrrhophus guttilatus*)

9. Dorsolateral folds present and extend well beyond
tympanum. . . . . Rio Grande Leopard Frog (*Rana berlandieri*)
Supratympanic folds present. . . . . .Bullfrog (*R. catesbeiana*)

GLOSSARY

amplexus   mating of anurans that involves the male tightly clasping the female prior to externally fertilizing her eggs.

anuran   a member of the order Anura; includes all frogs and toads.

axillary amplexus   mating position in which male clasps female around the waist just behind the forelimbs.

cranial crest   a bony ridge on the top or side of the head, present in many members of the family Bufonidae.

dentition   kind, number, and arrangement of teeth.

direct development   tadpole stage that takes place entirely within the egg; amphibians that have direct development do not require an aquatic environment for successful reproduction.

dorsal   on the back.

dorsolateral ridges   skin folds that extend longitudinally down the back of some frogs.

indirect development   progression from egg to frog that includes an aquatic tadpole stage before the juvenile and adult frog stages.

inguinal amplexus   mating position in which male clasps female around the waist or just in front of the hind limbs.

larval period   the time it takes for a tadpole to metamorphose from an egg into an adult frog or toad.

metatarsal tubercle   a small appendage on the hind foot of an anuran, often used for digging into the soil; also called a spade.

natural history   the study of living things in nature.

nuptial pads   enlarged pads present along the palm and thumb regions of many species of breeding male anurans.

oophagy   egg eating.

parotoid gland   a large glandular area behind the eye in some amphibian species; well developed in members of the family Bufonidae; its glandular secretions are toxic.

spade   see metatarsal tubercle.

supratympanic fold   skin fold that extends longitudinally above the eye and then vertically behind the tympanum of some frogs.

tinaja   bedrock pools where water will accumulate after rain.

tympanum   external auditory structure in anurans.

ventral   pertaining to the venter, or belly.

REFERENCES

Barber, P. H. 1999. Phylogeography of the Canyon Treefrog, *Hyla arenicolor* (Cope), Based on Mitochondrial DNA Sequence Data. *Molecular Ecology* 8:547–62.

Bury, R. B., and J. A. Whelan. 1984. Ecology and Management of the Bullfrog. *Resource Publication 155*. Washington, D.C.: U.S. Fish and Wildlife Service.

Conant, R., and J. T. Collins. 1998. *Reptiles and Amphibians of Eastern/Central North America*. 4th ed. Boston: Houghton Mifflin.

Crother, B. I., J. Boundy, J. A. Campbell, K. de Queiroz, D. R. Frost, R. Highton, J. B. Iverson, P. A. Meylan, T. W. Reeder, M. E. Seidel, J. W. Sites Jr., T. W. Taggart, S. G. Tilley, and D. B. Wake. 2000. Scientific and Standard English Names of Amphibians and Reptiles of North America North of Mexico, with Comments regarding Confidence in Our Understanding. *Society for the Study of Amphibians and Reptiles, Herpetological Circular* 29:1–82.

Dayton, G. H., and L. A. Fitzgerald. 2005. Priority Effects and Desert Anuran Communities. *Canadian Journal of Zoology* 83:1112–16.

Dayton, G. H., and S. D. Wapo. 2002. Cannibalistic Behavior in *Scaphiopus couchii:* More Evidence for Larval Anuran Oophagy. *Journal of Herpetology* 36:531–32.

Degenhardt, W. G., C. W. Painter, and A. H. Price. 1996. *Amphibians and Reptiles of New Mexico*. Albuquerque: University of New Mexico Press.

Dixon, J. R. 2000. *Amphibians and Reptiles of Texas*. College Station: Texas A&M University Press.

García-París, M., D. R. Buchholtz, and G. Parra-Olea. 2003. Phylogenetic Relationships of Pelobatoidea Re-examined Using mtDNA. *Molecular Phylogenetics and Evolution* 28:12–23.

Gehlbach, F. R. 1981. *Mountain Islands and Desert Seas: A Natural History of the U.S.-Mexican Borderlands*. College Station: Texas A&M University Press.

Heard, M. 1904. A California Frog Ranch. *Out West Magazine* 21:20–27.

Hunt, R. H. 1980. Toad Sanctuary in a Tarantula Burrow. *Natural History* 89:48–53.

Petranka, J. W., and C. A. Kennedy. 1999. Pond Tadpoles with Generalized Morphology: Is It Time to Reconsider Their Functional Roles in Aquatic Communities? *Oecologia* 120:621–31.

Pfennig, D. W. 1992. Proximate and Functional Causes of Polyphenism in an Anuran Tadpole. *Functional Ecology* 6:167–74.

Plumb, G. A. 1987. An Algorithmic Approach to Automated Vegetation Mapping of Big Bend National Park, Texas. Ph.D. diss., University of Kansas.

Stebbins, R. C. 1951. *Amphibians of Western North America.* Los Angeles: University of California Press.

———1985. *A Field Guide to Western Reptiles and Amphibians.* 2d ed. Boston: Houghton Mifflin.

Sullivan, B. K. 2005. *Bufo woodhousii.* In *Status and Conservation of U.S. Amphibians,* edited by M. J. Lannoo, 438–40. Berkeley: University of California Press.

Tevis, L. 1966. Unsuccessful Breeding by Desert Toads (*Bufo punctatus*) at the Limit of Their Ecological Tolerance. *Ecology* 47:766–75.

Zug, G. R., L. J. Vitt, and J. P. Caldwell. 2001. *Herpetology: An Introductory Biology of Amphibians and Reptiles.* San Diego: Academic Press.

INDEX